THE TOP SECRET BOOK OF PRACTICE ROUTINES

SHREDMENTOR
ROCK GUITAR ACADEMY

First edition published in 2019 by Jason Aaron Wood on behalf of ShredMentor Rock Guitar Academy.

Second edition reformatted, expanded & published in 2024 by Jason Aaron Wood on behalf of ShredMentor Rock Guitar Academy.

Copyright © by Jason Aaron Wood

All rights reserved. No part of this publication may be reproduced, stored in a retrieval system, or transmitted, in any form or by any means, electronic, mechanical, photocopying, recording or otherwise, without prior written permission in accordance with the Copyright Act of 1956 (as amended). Any person or persons who do any
unauthorized act in relation to this publication may be liable to criminal prosecution and civil claims for damages.

ISBN-13: 9798343124996

Printed in the USA.

CONTENTS

How Long to Spend on Each Skill 4
Technique Development vs Application 6
Speed Training: How It's Done 7
Full-Hour Templates: Overview 8
Half-Hour Templates: Overview 10
Full-Hour Templates 13
Half-Hour Templates 35
Power Up 47
Tips 49
Resources 56
What to Practice, Specifically 57
The 4 Pillars of T.A.D.S 62
The ShredMentor Strategies, Summarized... 67
The Layers of *True* Scale Knowledge.... 84
44 Essential Questions During Practice... 90
About the Author 98
Further Reading......................... 100

HOW LONG TO SPEND ON EACH SKILL?

DIFFERENT TYPES OF ACTIVITY REQUIRE DIFFERENT AMOUNTS OF TIME & FOCUS.

It's vital that you continually <u>apply</u> your skills in a musical way along to backing tracks, even if they're backing tracks you create yourself. Without interacting with other audible music, you'll only be able to understand what you're doing up to a certain extent.

All too often, guitarists spend ALL of their time in "exercise" mode, only practicing the guitar by itself without accompaniment. This is practicing in a controlled setting, like testing it out "in the lab."

It's essential that you also see how well you do in the real world, "in the field," identify what went wrong, & then take your findings back to "the lab," tweak as needed, try it again "in the field," and so on.

The goal in developing any skill is ultimately to be able to *actually use it* in a real life musical situation. It doesn't happen automatically though - you have to practice it that way.

| "Exercise" Mode
"IN THE LAB" | ⟷ | Musical Application
"IN THE FIELD" |

Get Your Custom Practice Strategy Now at **ShredMentor.com/strategy**

HOW LONG TO SPEND ON EACH SKILL?

3 to 5 minutes:
- Warmups
- Individual technique drills
- Individual sequences
- Planning specific altered-fingering patterns
- Trills (played _rhythmically_)
- Legato

10 to 15 minutes:
- Sequences in multiple modes
- Familiar Sweeping Patterns
- Mastering New Accenting Patterns w/ Alternate Picking
- Speed training on one exercise
  (see page 7)

15 to 20 minutes:
- Sweep Picking
  (_when new to the technique_)
- Ear Training along to a Drone or Backing Track
- Keeping some improvisation in regular rotation
  (_a few times through a 5- to 10-minute backing track_)

30 to 45 minutes:
- Learning songs or sections of songs
- Transcribing classical pieces from notation
- Practicing composing

melodies and harmonies
(while multi-track recording)

HOW MUCH PRACTICE TIME TO SPEND

DEVELOPING TECHNIQUE & VOCABULARY VS IMPROVISING TO BACKING TRACKS

Early in Vocabulary Development

- 66% "Exercise" Mode
- 34% Playing to Backing Tracks

Once Familiar with Roughly a Dozen Types of Phrases, Licks, and/or Sequences

- 50% "Exercise" Mode
- 50% Playing to Backing Tracks

Advanced Vocabulary, Practicing For Musicality

- 34% "Exercise" Mode
- 66% Playing to Backing Tracks

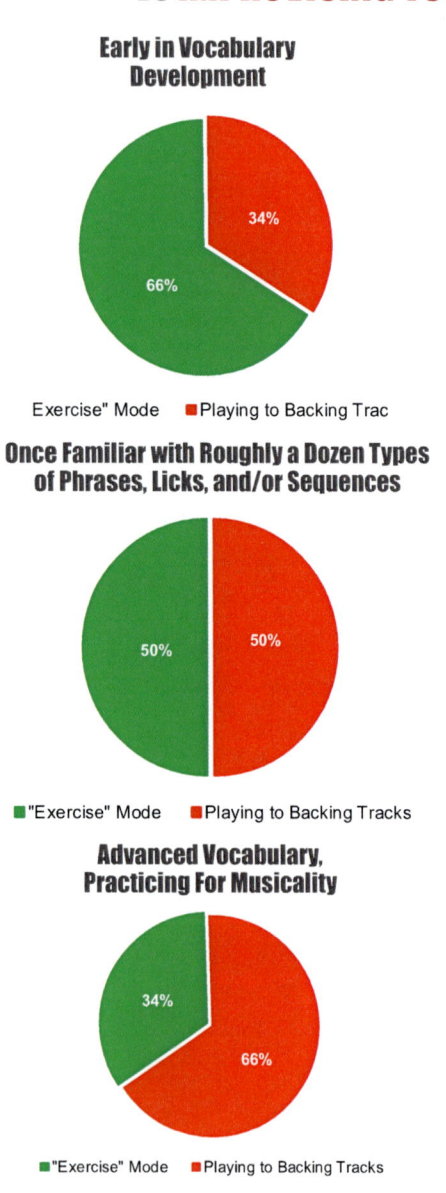

Obviously, you'll need to develop your technique to the highest level possible in order to be able to play
- anything you can imagine,
- at any tempo,
- on the spot.

But the huge mistake most guitarists make is <u>only</u> practicing technique in isolation, without practicing <u>using</u> the techniques they're working on in an actual musical situation.

Basically, the more vocabulary you acquire, the larger the portion of your practice time that should be devoted to *applying* it.

And hands-down, the best way to do that is using that vocabulary to **improvise along to backing tracks.**

The Top Secret Book of Practice Routines

SPEED TRAINING
HOW IT'S DONE

THERE ARE 5 SPEEDS, BUT YOU'LL ONLY USE 3:

~~Impossible:~~ Not challenging, because it's not even accessible.

Falling Apart: You can't even play more than 1 repetition at this speed without messing up. You're finding your current "ceiling" with this speed.

Tiring: You can feel your muscles getting tired as you progress; this is the feeling of your muscles developing. Work back to this speed & finish several repetitions here. This is the "sweet spot" where it's fast but you have control.

Easy: You can play it perfectly, but you have to concentrate to do so. Start here.

~~Effortless:~~ Not challenging, thus not benefitting you. Start faster than this.

EACH SKILL WILL HAVE ITS OWN 3 SPECIFIC BPM SPEEDS!

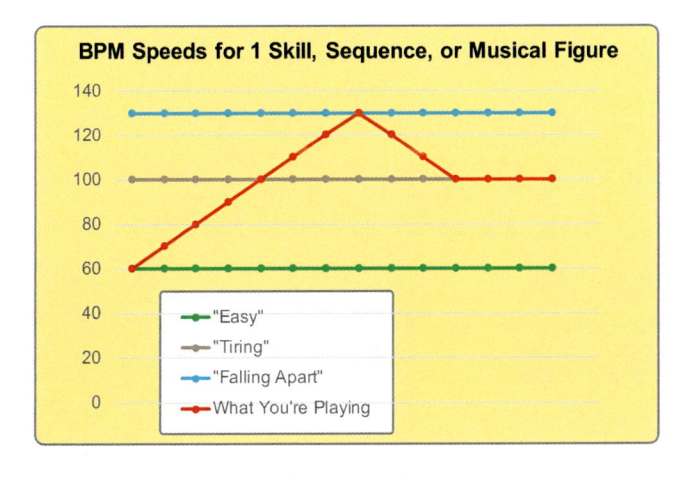

BPM Speeds for 1 Skill, Sequence, or Musical Figure

- "Easy"
- "Tiring"
- "Falling Apart"
- What You're Playing

One-Hour PRACTICE ROUTINE TEMPLATES
At-A-Glance

#1 — 6 SKILLS
- 10 min
- 10 min
- 10 min
- 10 min
- 10 min
- 10 min

#2 — 5 SKILLS
- 10 min
- 10 min
- 10 min
- 20 min
- 10 min

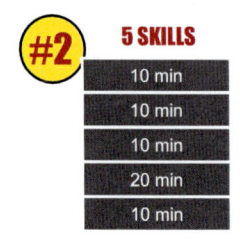

#3 — 10 SKILLS
- 3+3+3 min
- 10 min
- 20 min
- 3+3+3 min
- 5+5 min

#4 — 5 SKILLS
- 5 min
- 5 min
- 5 min
- 15 min
- 30 min

#5 — 4 SKILLS
- 5 min
- 5 min
- 5 min
- 45 min

#6 — 6 SKILLS
- 3 min
- 3 min
- 3 min
- 3 min
- 3 min

#7 — 7 SKILLS
- 3 min
- 3 min
- 3 min
- 3 min
- 3 min
- 15 min

#8 — 8 SKILLS
- 5+5+5 min
- 15 min
- 5+5+5 min
- 15 min

#9 — 9 SKILLS
- 3+3+3+3+3 min
- 5+5+5 min
- 30 min

#10 — 8 SKILLS
- 3+3+3+3+3 min
- 5 min
- 10 min
- 30 min

#11 — 7 SKILLS
- 5+5+5 min
- 10 min
- 15 min
- 15 min

#12 — 4 SKILLS
- 15 min
- 15 min
- 15 min
- 15 min

#13 — 3 SKILLS
20 min
20 min
20 min

#14 — 3 SKILLS
15 min
15 min
30 min

#15 — 3 SKILLS
3+3+3+3+3 min
5+5+5 min
30 min

#16 — 5 SKILLS
5+5+5+5 min
40 min

#17 — 5 SKILLS
5+5+5 min
10 min
15 min
15 min
5 min

#18 — 3 SKILLS
5 min
15 min
40 min

#19 — 4 SKILLS
10 min
15 min
15 min
20 min

Half-Hour PRACTICE ROUTINE TEMPLATES
At-A-Glance

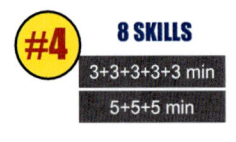

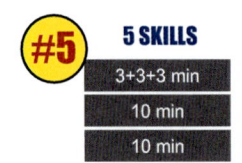

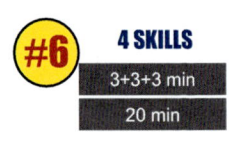

#1 — 3 SKILLS
- 10 min
- 10 min
- 10 min

#2 — 4 SKILLS
- 5 min
- 5 min
- 5 min
- 15 min

#3 — 6 SKILLS
- 3+3+3+3+3 min
- 15 min

#4 — 8 SKILLS
- 3+3+3+3+3 min
- 5+5+5 min

#5 — 5 SKILLS
- 3+3+3 min
- 10 min
- 10 min

#6 — 4 SKILLS
- 3+3+3 min
- 20 min

#7 — ANY/ALL SKILLS
- 30 min (all Improvisation, focusing on several different skills, combined.)

#8 — 3 SKILLS
- 5 min
- 5 min
- 20 min

#9 — 5 SKILLS
- 3 min
- 3 min
- 3 min
- 10 min
- 10 min

The Top Secret Book of Practice Routines

One-Hour
PRACTICE ROUTINE TEMPLATES

1 full hour is the ideal amount of time to practice every day, because it can accommodate a wide variety of different skill types, so you'll progress much faster by covering more ground every single day.

Therefore, try to devote an hour every day to practicing. Following are 19 different full-hour templates you can use to structure your practice time to get the fastest possible results.

Use a TIMER.

Don't keep looking at the clock to see how long it's been. That's a distraction from the actual task at hand.

Your playing requires 100% of your focus.

One-Hour PRACTICE ROUTINE TEMPLATE #1

THIS STRUCTURE IS BEST SUITED FOR:

6 SKILLS

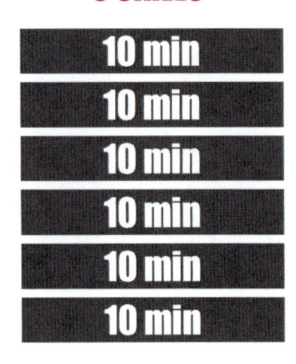

| 10 min |
| 10 min |
| 10 min |
| 10 min |
| 10 min |
| 10 min |

An easy-to-follow, simple breakdown of an hour into 6 segments.

- Great for speed training in any/all of the 6 time segments.

- Taking on new sequences in at least 3 adjacent modes of a given scale

- Sweeping patterns (once familiar)

- Mastering new accenting patterns w/ alternate picking

- Speed training on any one of these exercises.

One-Hour PRACTICE ROUTINE TEMPLATE #2

THIS STRUCTURE IS BEST SUITED FOR:

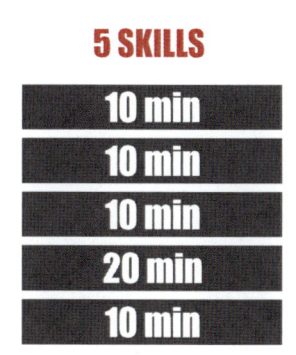

5 SKILLS
- 10 min
- 10 min
- 10 min
- 20 min
- 10 min

Speed Training in 4 Different Skills, *plus 20 Minutes of Improvising* Along to Backing Tracks, or Sweeping.

- Taking on new Sequences in at least 3 adjacent modes of a given scale in each exercise (10 minutes per sequence)

- Sweeping patterns (once familiar), especially multiple arpeggios practiced as chord progressions.

- Mastering new accenting patterns w/ alternate picking

- Speed training on one exercise

- Practicing 4 skills, then spending 20 min. applying them by improvising along to backing tracks, with 10 final min spent going over rough spots.

One-Hour PRACTICE ROUTINE TEMPLATE #3

THIS STRUCTURE IS BEST SUITED FOR:

10 SKILLS

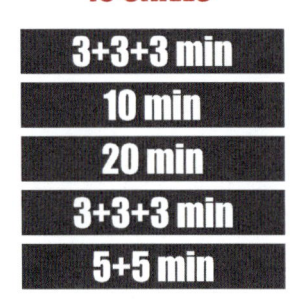

3+3+3 min
10 min
20 min
3+3+3 min
5+5 min

Yes, 3+3+3 = 9, not 10. Close enough. Take a 1 minute break afterwards, or make it 3 minutes & 20 seconds each.

Maintenance, Speed Training & Musical Application via Improvisation.

- Maintenance in 3 areas already familiar/established.

- Speed training, learning a new sequence, or complicated picking patterns.

- Improvising to backing tracks.

- Maintenance in 3 additional familiar areas/skills.

- Picking Speed, Legato, or Maintenance in 2 other areas that are:
    - More difficult, and/or
    - Combinations of other skills (e.g., *Sequence of 3rds* and *Sequence of Fours* combined back-to-back)

One-Hour
PRACTICE ROUTINE TEMPLATE #4

THIS STRUCTURE IS BEST SUITED FOR:

5 SKILLS

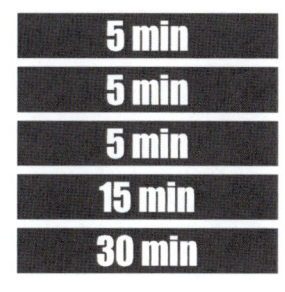

| 5 min |
| 5 min |
| 5 min |
| 15 min |
| 30 min |

Combined Maintenance of Established Skills, Expansion into New Vocabulary, & Musical Application/Integration of Skills.

- Maintenance & further development in 3 areas that are already somewhat familiar for 5 minutes each.

- Sweeping familiar arpeggio patterns, taking on a new unfamiliar scale (in fragments, rhythmically), or speed training in either 2 easier patterns or 1 long and complex one for 15 minutes.

- Applying the above skills along to a backing track, or learning parts of a song (or playing all the way through songs you already know).

One-Hour
PRACTICE ROUTINE TEMPLATE #5

THIS STRUCTURE IS BEST SUITED FOR:

4 SKILLS

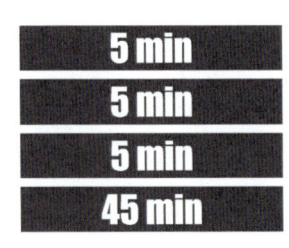

5 min
5 min
5 min
45 min

Warmup & Maintenance in 3 Areas, with a Primary Focus on Improvisation & Being Musical.

- Maintenance & further development in **3 areas** that are already somewhat familiar for 5 minutes each. The first of these can also serve as a warmup.

- Applying the above skills along to a backing track & really working through your phrasing & expression, writing/recording and working with melody and harmony, or learning how to play a song.

One-Hour
PRACTICE ROUTINE TEMPLATE   #6

THIS STRUCTURE IS BEST SUITED FOR:

6 SKILLS

| 3 min |
| 3 min |
| 3 min |
| 3 min |
| 3 min |
| 45 min |

Warmup & Maintenance in 5 Very Familiar/ Established Areas, with a Primary Focus on Improvisation & Being Musical.

- Maintenance & further development in **5 areas** that are already somewhat familiar, in rapid-fire fashion for 3 minutes each. The first one or two of these can also serve as a warmup.

- Applying the above skills along to a backing track & really working through your phrasing & expression, writing/recording and working with melody and harmony, or learning how to play a song.

One-Hour
PRACTICE ROUTINE TEMPLATE #7

THIS STRUCTURE IS BEST SUITED FOR:

7 SKILLS

- 3 min
- 3 min
- 3 min
- 3 min
- 3 min
- 15 min
- 30 min

Warmup & Maintenance in 5 Very Familiar/Established Skills, with a Primary Focus on Improvisation & Being Musical with Them.

- Maintenance & further development in **5 areas** that are already familiar, in rapid-fire fashion for 3 minutes each.

- Speed training in 2 easier skills or 1 complex one, sweep arpeggios, or taking on a new sequence and/or scale type for 15 minutes.

- Applying the above skills along to a backing track & really working through your phrasing & expression, writing/recording and working with melody and harmony, or learning how to play a song.

One-Hour PRACTICE ROUTINE TEMPLATE #8

THIS STRUCTURE IS BEST SUITED FOR:

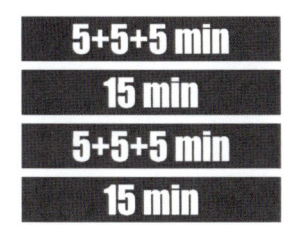

8 SKILLS
- 5+5+5 min
- 15 min
- 5+5+5 min
- 15 min

Warmup & Maintenance in 3 Familiar/Established Skills with Musical Application. Then Repeat with 3 Other Skills.

- Maintenance & further development in **3 areas** that are already somewhat familiar, in rapid-fire fashion for 5 minutes each.

- Speed training in 2 easier skills or 1 complex one, taking on a new sequence and/or scale type for 15 minutes.

- Maintenance & further development in **3 additional areas** that are already familiar, in rapid-fire fashion for 5 minutes each.

- Applying each set of 3 skills along to a backing track with phrasing & expression for 15 minutes.

One-Hour
PRACTICE ROUTINE TEMPLATE #9

THIS STRUCTURE IS BEST SUITED FOR:

9 SKILLS

- 3+3+3+3+3 min
- 5+5+5 min
- 30 min

Warmup & Maintenance in 8 Familiar/ Established Areas, with Equal Focus on Improvisation & Being Musical with Those Skills.

- Maintenance & further development in 5 very familiar areas, in rapid-fire fashion for 3 minutes each.

- Maintenance & further development in 3 additional familiar areas that are somewhat more difficult, in rapid-fire fashion for 5 minutes each.

- Applying the above skills along to a backing track with phrasing & expression.

The Top Secret Book of Practice Routines

One-Hour PRACTICE ROUTINE TEMPLATE #10

THIS STRUCTURE IS BEST SUITED FOR:

8 SKILLS

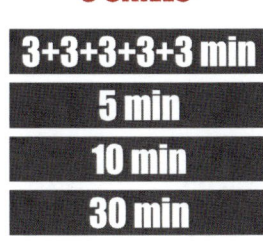

| 3+3+3+3+3 min |
| 5 min |
| 10 min |
| 30 min |

Rapid-Fire Warmup & Maintenance in 5 Familiar/Established Areas, 5 Minutes of Legato, 1 Speed Training Session, & Equal Focus on Improvisation & Being Musical.

- Maintenance & further development in 5 very familiar areas, in rapid-fire fashion for 3 minutes each.

- Maintenance & further development in 1 additional familiar area – perfect for pure legato -- for 5 minutes.

- Speed training for 10 minutes on one skill.

- Applying the above skills along to a backing track with phrasing & expression.

One-Hour
PRACTICE ROUTINE TEMPLATE #11

THIS STRUCTURE IS BEST SUITED FOR:

7 SKILLS

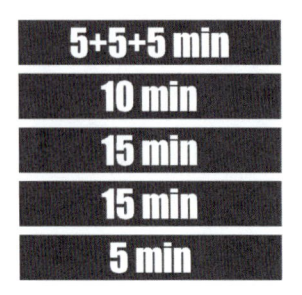

| 5+5+5 min |
| 10 min |
| 15 min |
| 15 min |
| 5 min |

Pure Technique/Fretboard Development, with Warmup, Maintenance, Speed Training, Sweep Picking & Legato.

- Maintenance & further development in 3 familiar areas, in rapid-fire fashion for 5 minutes each.

- Speed training for 10 minutes on one skill.

- Speed training in 2 additional, more difficult skills or a more complex sequence for 15 minutes each. Or, tackling sweep arpeggios for one or both of these 15 minute segments.

- Finish off with purely hammer-ons & pull-offs for 5 minutes.

One-Hour
PRACTICE ROUTINE TEMPLATE #12

THIS STRUCTURE IS BEST SUITED FOR:

4 SKILLS

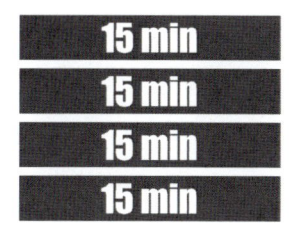

- 15 min
- 15 min
- 15 min
- 15 min

A Well-Balanced Routine Focused on Technique, Phrasing, Speed & Application/Improvisation.

- Warming up with a skill for 5 minutes then speed training with the same skill for the following 10 minutes. Or, speed training in one or more complex musical figure or sequence.

- Sweep arpeggio practice.

- Working on phrasing skills like various string-bending techniques, your vibrato quality, sliding accuracy, and more.

- Put these skills & patterns to the test along to a backing track, with extra emphasis on maintaining expressive phrasing.

One-Hour
PRACTICE ROUTINE TEMPLATE #13

THIS STRUCTURE IS BEST SUITED FOR:

3 SKILLS

20 min
20 min
20 min

A Well-Balanced Routine Focused on Difficult Technique and/or Unfamiliar Scales & Shapes, Phrasing, & Application/ Improvisation.

- Learning new sweep arpeggios or getting started with sweep picking, or learning a new scale and/or other difficult skill.

- Working on phrasing skills like various string-bending techniques, your vibrato quality, sliding accuracy, and more.

- Put these skills & patterns to the test along to a backing track, with extra emphasis on maintaining expressive phrasing.

One-Hour
PRACTICE ROUTINE TEMPLATE #14

THIS STRUCTURE IS BEST SUITED FOR:

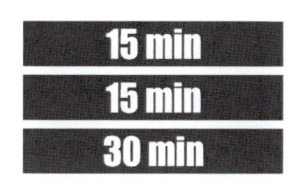

3 SKILLS
- 15 min
- 15 min
- 30 min

Split focus on Technique with Speed Training, and on Musical Application of Your Skills.

- <u>Two</u> mini speed training sessions on more complex musical figures.

- Or, one speed training segment for 15 minutes, then practice phrasing techniques (like consistent bending intonation, sliding technique accuracy, or vibrato quality) for the next 15 minute segment.

- Put these & other skills & patterns to the test by improvising with them along to backing tracks, with extra emphasis on maintaining expressive phrasing.

One-Hour PRACTICE ROUTINE TEMPLATE #15

THIS STRUCTURE IS BEST SUITED FOR:

3 SKILLS

- 10 min
- 20 min
- 30 min

Technique/Speed, Something New, & Musical Application of Your Skills.

- Speed training on one skill or musical figure, potentially using multiple modes.

- Taking on a new skill like sweep picking or economy picking, or tackling a new type of scale or other fretboard pattern; working on creating a new tapping pattern, or modulating any of these to follow a specific chord progression. Also great for ear training and/or honing the exactness of your bending technique along to a backing drone.

- Put these & other skills & patterns to the test along to a backing track for the second half or your practice session.

One-Hour
PRACTICE ROUTINE TEMPLATE #16

THIS STRUCTURE IS BEST SUITED FOR:

5 SKILLS

5+5+5+5 min

40 min

4 Areas of Warmup/ Maintenance, with a Heavy Focus on Improvisation & Musical Application.

- Choose 4 skills that are already familiar to keep in rotation, and in rapid-fire fashion, run through them for 5 minutes each. The first one or two can also serve as a warmup if you start with the easiest ones.

- For the remaining 40 minutes, focus your attention on applying those techniques together, with phrasing, along to one or more backing tracks.

  PRO TIP: Try different tempos every 10 to 20 minutes to compare/contrast what it feels like and where your limits are.

One-Hour
PRACTICE ROUTINE TEMPLATE #17

THIS STRUCTURE IS BEST SUITED FOR:

5 SKILLS

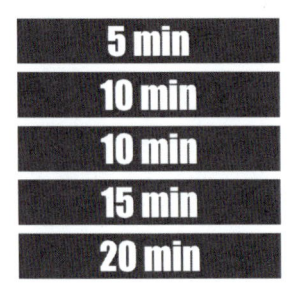

- 5 min
- 10 min
- 10 min
- 15 min
- 20 min

A well-rounded practice session with a warmup, speed/technique development, & musical application via improvisation.

- Warm up for 5 minutes with something familiar. Diving in with speed picking/tremolo picking along to double-bass beats can really set the energy level for the whole session.

- Two 10 minute segments of speed training in a reasonably easy or familiar pattern, and one 15 minute segment focused on either speed training with a more complicated musical figure, or on sweep arpeggios, a new alternate picking challenge, or fragments of an unfamiliar scale.

- For the final 20 minutes, focus on applying these same skills while improvising along to a backing track. Try switching tempos 10 minutes in by using a different backing track (for an extra challenge, change keys too).

One-Hour
PRACTICE ROUTINE TEMPLATE #18

THIS STRUCTURE IS BEST SUITED FOR:

3 SKILLS

- 5 min
- 15 min
- 40 min

A warmup, one particular technique focus for the day (with speed training if desired), & the primary focus on applying it musically.

- Warm up for 5 minutes with something familiar. Diving in with speed picking/tremolo picking along to double-bass beats can really set the energy level for the whole session.

- Choose one main technique and practice it for 15 minutes; push your speed in this technique to maximize the number of situations and tempos when you can use it.

- For the final 40 minutes, focus on applying this same skill within your normal playing style while improvising along to a backing track. Try switching tempos every 10 to 20 minutes by using a different backing track (for an extra challenge, change keys too).

One-Hour
PRACTICE ROUTINE TEMPLATE #19

THIS STRUCTURE IS BEST SUITED FOR:

4 SKILLS

| 10 min |
| 15 min |
| 15 min |
| 20 min |

Developing Speed for 3 Techniques & Then Musically Applying Them & Improvising with Them.

- Speed training on 1 relatively simple musical figure, then on either 4 more simple ones (7.5 minutes each, breaking each 15 minute segment in half) or 2 more complex ones (15 minutes each).

- For the final 20 minutes, focus on applying these same skills together by improvising along to one or two backing tracks.

33

Half-Hour PRACTICE ROUTINE TEMPLATES

While a full hour is ideal, and you should try to devote an hour per day to practice, you can still cover a bit of ground on days when you can only devote a half hour to practicing.

Following are several half-hour templates you can use to maximize your results when you only have a half hour available to practice.

Half-Hour PRACTICE ROUTINE TEMPLATE #1

THIS STRUCTURE IS BEST SUITED FOR:

3 SKILLS
- 10 min
- 10 min
- 10 min

An easy-to-follow, simple breakdown of a half hour into 3 segments. Great for speed training in any/all of the 3 areas.

- Taking on new sequences in at least 3 adjacent modes

- Sweeping patterns (once familiar)

- Mastering new accenting patterns w/ alternate picking

- Speed training on any one of these exercises.

Half-Hour
PRACTICE ROUTINE TEMPLATE #2

THIS STRUCTURE IS BEST SUITED FOR:

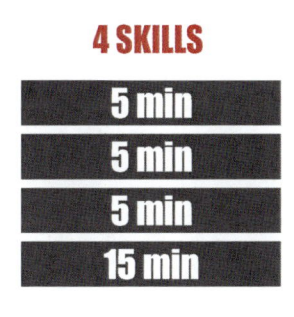

4 SKILLS

| 5 min |
| 5 min |
| 5 min |
| 15 min |

Warmup & Maintenance in 3 Areas, with Equal Focus on Improvisation & Being Musical.

- Maintenance & further development in 3 areas that are already somewhat familiar for 5 minutes each.

- Applying the above skills along to a backing track & using them expressively.

Half-Hour PRACTICE ROUTINE TEMPLATE #3

THIS STRUCTURE IS BEST SUITED FOR:

6 SKILLS
3+3+3+3+3 min
15 min

Warmup & Maintenance in 5 Areas, While Equally Focusing on Improvisation & Being Musical.

- Maintenance & further development in 5 areas that are already quite familiar or fairly easy, for 3 minutes each.

- Applying the above skills along to a backing track & using them expressively.

Half-Hour
PRACTICE ROUTINE TEMPLATE   #4

THIS STRUCTURE IS BEST SUITED FOR:

8 SKILLS
3+3+3+3+3 min
5+5+5 min

Pure Technique & Ongoing Sequence Vocabulary Work.

- Maintenance & further development in 5 areas that are already quite familiar or fairly easy, in rapid-fire fashion for 3 minutes each.

- Maintenance & further development in 3 other more difficult and/or less-familiar areas for 5 minutes each.

The Top Secret Book of Practice Routines

Half-Hour PRACTICE ROUTINE TEMPLATE #5

THIS STRUCTURE IS BEST SUITED FOR:

5 SKILLS

3+3+3 min
10 min
10 min

Technique/Vocabulary Maintenance plus Speed Training.

- Maintenance & further development in 3 areas that are already quite familiar or fairly easy, in rapid-fire fashion for 3 minutes each.

- Speed training in 2 successive musical figures or sequences, or in 1 of them, and the other 10 minutes spent improvising with today's skills along to a backing track.

Half-Hour
PRACTICE ROUTINE TEMPLATE #6

THIS STRUCTURE IS BEST SUITED FOR:

4 SKILLS

3+3+3 min
20 min

Technique/Vocabulary Maintenance plus Musical Application.

- Maintenance & further development in 3 areas that are already quite familiar or fairly easy, in rapid-fire fashion for 3 minutes each.

- 20 minutes spent improvising, especially focusing on today's skills, along to a backing track.

Half-Hour
PRACTICE ROUTINE TEMPLATE #7

THIS STRUCTURE IS BEST SUITED FOR:

ANY/ALL SKILLS

30 min
(all improvisation, focusing on several different skills, combined.)

Pure Musical Application of What You've Developed So Far.

- Crank up the backing tracks & start being musical! Intentionally think of some of the techniques that are a high priority & work them in - & also *purposely combine several techniques* as you play.

- Focus especially on how accurate your bending is & how expressive & consistent your vibrato is throughout the session.

- Pay close attention to which notes from the scale to land on (which ones resolve to the chord), depending on which chord is playing at the moment.

Half-Hour
PRACTICE ROUTINE TEMPLATE   #8

THIS STRUCTURE IS BEST SUITED FOR:

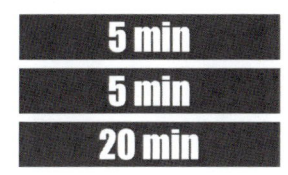

3 SKILLS
- 5 min
- 5 min
- 20 min

Warmup/Maintenance in 2 Areas, Followed by Musical Application of Them.

- Choose 2 fairly familiar skills to continue developing, spending 5 minutes on each.

- Using backing tracks, work both of those skills/techniques in as much as you can, along with the things you already do well. Stay focused on expressive phrasing throughout.

Half-Hour PRACTICE ROUTINE TEMPLATE #9

THIS STRUCTURE IS BEST SUITED FOR:

5 SKILLS

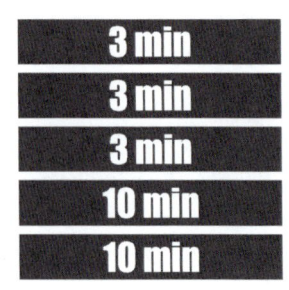

3 min
3 min
3 min
10 min
10 min

Warmup/Maintenance in 3 Areas, With Speed Training & Optional Musical Application.

- Choose 3 familiar skills to continue developing, spending 3 minutes on each one, back-to-back in rapid-fire fashion.

- Choose 2 patterns for speed training, for 10 minutes each.

- Optionally, instead, only do speed training for the first 10 minute segment, then spend the last 10 minutes intentionally using today's skills along to a backing track. Stay focused on expressive phrasing throughout.

POWER UP:

Even using these powerful templates, it's <u>*vital*</u> that you realize that *practicing just one way all the time* <u>will</u> start to slow down your progress.

Here's why...

When you practice the *same things*, the *same way*, over & over, you're eventually just covering the same ground, which causes you to stop challenging your <u>mind</u> to solve the problems that come with tackling new approaches.

That's why after about a week, you should **change which template you're following**, & shift your focus to other areas of development.

Do this every week so your progress doesn't stagnate & your mind stays freshly challenged.

Or, even **schedule a full week's worth of practice routines at a time, using _several different practice routine templates_** to cover an even wider, more diverse range of musical skills.

TIPS FOR MORE PRODUCTIVE PRACTICE

So far we've covered quite a few different ways of approaching practicing, based on what your goals are & how much time you have available to practice.

In the following several pages, you'll find powerful tips to get the ***absolute maximum benefit*** when practicing for each area of development.

WARMUPS
LOOSE MUSCLES & A MOTIVATING ENERGY LEVEL

- Gently stretch before you start practicing, *especially* if you are planning on doing any speed training – you can seriously injure yourself if you skip this step!

- Turn on a practice beat and start jamming along to it. Don't necessarily even avoid the higher tempos, as they will more likely set a higher energy level at the start of the practice session and leave you feeling pumped and energized.

- Picking speed is another great way to start off and set a high energy level for the session.

RAPID-FIRE DRILLS
KEEPING WHAT YOU'VE DEVELOPED IN REGULAR ROTATION

- Use a timer to keep track of how long it's been — 3 & 5 minute time intervals are over before you know it.

- You can even use **Hyper** or another productivity timer app on your smart phone to keep your session structured. (*No affiliation - it's just really cool and helpful.*)

- These are especially great for covering basic sequences once you're familiar with them. Start at one mode of the scale, move up a mode, back down to the original mode, then down one mode again — that's "one time" through the idea, and it greatly strengthens your fretboard knowledge as well as your technique & motor memory.

SPEED TRAINING

MAXIMIZING THE NUMBER OF SITUATIONS WHEN YOU CAN USE YOUR SKILLS

- It's not just about showing off or the intensity of speed – your speed actually determines how many of the things you know how to do are even *accessible* at certain tempos. Some things just become impossible when the tempo reaches a certain point.

- **Rhythmic Theme of the Day:** choose one time signature and rhythmic sub-beat value and stick with it the whole day. You may even want to stick with it for a whole week. This makes it so that <u>everything you play can be used together</u> and dropped right into a riff or solo, and it can all even be used in the same song if desired.

- Metronomes are okay, but practicing to programmed drum beats is much more effective and musical. And for speed, nothing beats double-bass drum beats.

MORE ON
SPEED TRAINING

MAXIMIZING THE NUMBER OF SITUATIONS WHEN YOU CAN USE YOUR SKILLS

- If you make a mistake at a specific speed, let the beat keep playing and start the drill over until you're satisfied you did it the best you can, before moving on.

- Don't beat yourself up over mistakes, but don't ignore them either. <u>Identify what's causing them</u> and pay extra attention in those moments to overcome them. They're usually "tendencies" based on habits, so paying closer attention to those details usually gets rid of them.

- In general, 4 repetitions of the musical figure, plus a final note, is a good guideline, per BPM.

- Add a final note and use it as an opportunity to include bending & vibrato: a graceful ending is everything! Speed counts for *nothing* if the ending is a mess.

IMPROVISATION

HOW WELL CAN YOU USE YOUR SKILLS WHEN IT MATTERS WHICH NOTE YOU HIT AT WHICH TIME?

- Always listen to & identify exactly what the chord progression IS before you start playing over it. Also identify which notes from the scale make up each chord in the progression.

- In fact, don't play "over" the chord progression at all – play "<u>within</u>" it. Your notes become <u>part</u> of the chord: you're either (A) reinforcing one of the notes already in the chord, or you're (B) adding a new note to it, making it a new type of chord. So pay close attention to how your "ingredients" mix with what's already there.

- Follow what the drums are doing. If the drums are already playing a certain groove, play with your accents in at least some of the same places. If they go off into a drum roll, that's a perfect time to match them with a phrase or phrases that follow the exact same rhythm (or very close).

USE THE RIGHT TOOLS

SET YOURSELF UP TO SUCCEED BY USING THE RIGHT TOOLS FOR THE RIGHT MUSICAL SITUATIONS

ShredMentor.com features a huge library of 3 different kinds of backing tracks: drum beats, chord progressions, and drones. Each is for a specific purpose:

- **Beats:** Speed, Syncopation, Rhythmic Tightness, Syncopation, Polymeter & Polyrhythms, Improvising Rhythmic Grooves & Riffs, Jamming with Others

- **Chord Progressions:** Fluid melodic improvising, Chord Tone Targeting, Chord Melody/Voice Leading, Modulating Sequences, Phrasing, Active Listening, Assessing Where You Need Further Speed Development

- **Drones:** Ear Training, Bending Accuracy, Learning What Each Note of a Given Scale Does Within the Overall Harmony, Understanding Modes, Practicing Playing Over 1 Specific Chord from a Given Key

These are also available at **https://shredmentor.bandcamp.com**.

RESOURCES

EXPERIENCE THE SHREDMENTOR DIFFERENCE

- **ShredMentor.com**
  Home of the **Total Artist Development System**, ShredMentor.com is THE place to go for the ultimate in guitar lessons & training if you want to become self-sufficient as a musician, especially if you love metal, hard rock, soloing, or shred, and neoclassical shred in particular.

  After our Initial Strategy Session, I'll create a 100% personalized strategy based on achieving your specific goals in the fastest time possible.

  This is also where you'll find the powerful **Guitar Practice Tools**, featuring hundreds of backing tracks, diagrams & other tools to challenge you in ways that count in real-life musical situations. Plus, 201 free Challenge of the Day videos, with tab, and a growing library of lesson packs.

- **ShredMentor.Bandcamp.com**
  Most of the backing tracks from ShredMentorOnline.com, for sale in digital album format at extremely low prices.

- **YouTube.com/ShredMentor**
  Loads of useful videos, including 201 free "Challenge of the Day" video lessons (great for individual skills to apply with the templates in this book!), and 79 full-hour episodes of ShredMentor LIVE!, a live streaming weekly guitar that Jason ran between late 2021 to mid 2023.

- **The Book of Sequences**
  A book devoted to the art of not only melody writing, but to creating your own exercises, riffs, & solos as well.

- **The Solo Writing Notebook**
  The ultimate creativity tool for the aspiring lead guitarist, designed to help you keep track of all the music theory concepts you need to balance while writing solos. It's like a blank tab book on steroids!

- **1,001 Guitar Practice Ideas**
  With this 101-page book in your arsenal, it'll be a long time before you can't figure out what to work on. With 1,001 things to jog your memory & spur your creativity, you'll also find quite a few extra practice tips scattered throughout the book.

THE "SKILLS" YOUR PRACTICE SHOULD CONSIST OF, SPECIFICALLY

TECHNIQUES
FOR THE PICKING HAND

- **All Down-Strokes:** Your ability to play successive down-strokes evenly is vital for certain styles of riffing, and it actually plays a significant role in speed picking with alternate picking.

- **Alternate Picking, Tremolo Picking, & Strumming:** These are the default picking techniques. Devote a portion of your time to mastering them.

- **Sweep Picking & Economy Picking:** Both are forms of Directional Picking, & in certain cases they will allow you to pick a series of notes with a single, flowing pick stroke. Must be tailored to the situation, unlike Alternate Picking, which can technically be used to play literally anything.

- **String Skipping:** When your notes aren't on adjacent strings, hitting the right string becomes significantly more difficult.

- **Hybrid Picking & Fingerpicking:** Using spare fingers on your picking hand can allow you to access melodies that would be extremely difficult, if not impossible, otherwise, & fingerpicking puts up to 5 different notes within reach instantly.

- **Tapping & Multi-Finger Tapping:** When you run out of fingers on your fretting hand, you still have several more, which enable you to play much wider intervals.

- **Pinch Harmonics:** A well-placed "squeal" falls under the domain of the picking hand as well.

- **Palm Muting & String Noise Control:** Getting a great tone & having control with selective palm muting is vital for expression. Keeping unwanted string noise to a minimum is also largely controlled by the picking hand.

TECHNIQUES
FOR THE FRETTING HAND

- **Hammer-Ons & Pull-Offs:** The ultimate strength & accuracy builders for fretting hand technique, since the fingers not only have to land in the right place, but do so strongly enough to actually sound the note - & with the exact right timing.

- **Scale Patterns & Their Modes:** The most valuable motor memory patterns you can learn are based on the scales you'll use the most. Your fingers need to learn their movements based on these interval spacings, from every note in the scale.

- **Arpeggios:** Whether sweeping, using hammer-ons & pull-offs, alternate picking, tapping, or any combination of these techniques, arpeggios outline the harmony for every note in the key, & they're essential for making sure your melodies don't consist solely of boring, predictable "linear" scale runs.

- **String Skipping:** Just as much of a challenge for the fretting hand, it's also a whole category of fretboard vocabulary unto itself.

- **Chord Shapes & Switching Between Chords:** Every single transition from one chord to another requires a specific series of coordinated movements that need to be executed gracefully.

- **Wide-Interval Stretching:** Using one finger per fret is a good guideline when you're starting out, but it's extremely limiting. Learning to stretch to play wider intervals with control is absolutely essential & exponentially broadens your melodic options.

- **Natural Harmonics:** Knowing the locations on the string where harmonics are located adds an entirely new texture to your arsenal.

- **Strummed Octaves & General Intervals:** Strumming octaves of the same note create powerful "single-note" melodies to layer into your rhythm guitar parts. For that matter, every other interval has its own sound as well, so learn their shapes and finger combinations by heart.

PHRASING TECHNIQUES

FOR MAXIMUM EXPRESSION

- **String Bending:** This is easily one of the most versatile techniques, bending is also one of the most expressive. Bending, bend & release, pre-bend & release, unison bend, double-stop bend, & rhythmically bending between notes of your melody - they all give you a distinctive character that make your melodies much more exciting than if you were to just play all your notes at their "home frets."

- **Vibrato:** To truly make your notes sing, you've got to develop control of the speed & width of your bends while performing vibrato, not to mention purposely waiting 1 to 2 beats before beginning to apply vibrato to a note.

- **Sliding:** Similar to how you might use string bending, sliding also allows you to "glide" to much wider intervals than bending would allow, & comes with the added benefit of relocating your hand to a different position of the fretboard.

- **Syncopation:** Interesting music doesn't always start on the down beat & end on another down beat. Emphasizing up beats & starting & ending your melodies in less predictable places will get your listener moving & add life to your music.

- **The "3 Textures":** Being able to morph between legato, picking, and selective palm muting at will, will keep the listener on the edge of their seat. Practice this with the same melody, switching to the next texture after 2 to 4 repetitions.

- **Trills, Turns, Mordents & Other Ornamentation:** Thrown in at just the right time, these can add a touch of magic to your melodies.

- **Natural & Pinch Harmonics:** A well-played, clear harmonic at the right time can add an almost otherworldly power to what you play, especially with a touch of tasteful vibrato added to it.

TAKE YOUR MUSICIANSHIP EVEN FURTHER

If you've come this far in this book, you're already committed to maximizing your practice time and accelerating your growth as a musician.

But there's so much more waiting for you beyond efficient practice—there's the potential to truly flourish in your musicianship.

That's where the **Total Artist Development System** (*TADS*) and its **4 Pillars** come into play, opening the door to exponential growth.

Most of the book up until now has focused primarily on Pillars 1 and 2: Technique & Vocabulary, and Improvisation.

But true mastery demands more, and it's essential to always be working with at least 2 of these 4 Pillars in tandem.

Let's break down the incredible impact that working across these 4 Pillars can have on your musicianship:

Technique practice informs and defines your essential playing **vocabulary**. The vocabulary of music is built on the techniques you practice and refine daily. The better your command over these techniques, the larger your musical "word bank" becomes, empowering you to express a broader range of musical ideas.

Improvisation creates fluency, transcending rote repetition. When you apply those techniques while improvising over backing tracks, you move beyond practicing in isolation—you develop the ability to adapt in real time. Improvisation is where your vocabulary starts to breathe, evolve, and transform into fluent, musical conversation. It's where you break free from robotic repetition and enter a space of genuine, on-the-spot expression. In fact, musical inprovisation is really spontaneous composing!

Songwriting & Recording become seamless extensions of your skillset. Mastery of the first two Pillars forms a rock-solid foundation for Pillar 3: Songwriting & Recording. Strong technique, broad vocabulary, and fluency turn the writing and recording process into an almost effortless experience. Imagine hitting "record" and improvising your way through entire sections of songs—every take being musical and meaningful, potentially a keeper. With this level of proficiency, recording an album is no longer an overwhelming chore, but an exciting creative outlet where even spontaneous performances yield album-

The Music Industry: Understanding your role and thriving. The final, often overlooked aspect of being a musician is navigating the music industry. Pillar 4, The Music Industry, is where you learn how things really work—gaining the insights and tools necessary to find your place within this vast landscape. This understanding is crucial to ensuring that your journey is rewarding rather than frustrating or disillusioning. The skills you need to thrive in the industry—whether marketing yourself, negotiating opportunities, or connecting with audiences—become new avenues for creativity and growth, sharpening your vision as an artist.

Working Across the 4 Pillars

The beauty of TADS lies in its interconnectedness.

These 4 Pillars aren't isolated; they form a powerful pipeline designed to transform you into a well-rounded musician.

When you actively engage with multiple Pillars, you build not only technical proficiency but also a deep understanding of the craft — as well as the business — of music, accelerating your growth exponentially.

TADS isn't just about developing skills—it's about helping you identify your specific challenges and strategically target your needs as a musician.

For the 5+ years I spent developing TADS, my aim was always to develop a training program that achieves the perfect balance of all aspects of musicianship that you need in place in order to hold your own in the real world of the music industry.

Up to now in this book, we've discussed concepts for practice and personal development. But as we move forward, let's delve into specific strategies that can help propel your growth even further.

And by "strategy," I'm about to get very specific.

In the next section, I'm going to share a summary of the **47 ShredMentor Strategies** that I've developed over the years to help guitarists like you overcome obstacles and become the musicians they've always envisioned themselves becoming.

> The full book, **The ShredMentor Strategies**, goes far more in-depth on each strategy, how, when and why to use each one, which ones work especially well together, and examples of what they would look like in real life.

The Top Secret Book of Practice Routines

THE SHRED MENTOR STRATEGIES SUMMARIZED

THE SHREDMENTOR STRATEGIES (SUMMARIZED)

In this section, I'll share what I've never shared in its entirety before, even in this brief summarized form. I've hesitated to share this information publicly for years, given how powerful these strategies are.

But with this 2nd edition of The Top Secret Book of Practice Routines, I wanted to add so much more value and give you the tools to really start seeing, hearing, and feeling more significant results from your playing right away, so that desire ultimately outweighed my desire to keep my trade secrets to myself.

Each of these strategies is built into the Total Artist Development System, and some appear directly on the personalized practice routines I create for not only my students, but for my own practice routines.

STRUCTURED PRACTICE & LEARNING
THE STRUCTURED TIME STRATEGY
The Structured Time Strategy emphasizes the importance of breaking down practice time into segments to focus on multiple skills rather than obsessing over one particular skill. This enables you to cover exponentially more areas of development in a single practice session than you would otherwise.

THE RHYTHMIC THEME OF THE DAY STRATEGY
(Compatible-Vocabulary-Based Training)
The Rhythmic Theme of the Day Strategy focuses on practicing phrases that are rhythmically compatible, concentrating on rhythms based on "threes" and "fours" to develop a versatile vocabulary. By practicing in these rhythmic contexts, guitarists can build a strong

foundation that enables them to play various phrases on the spot, broadening their skill set without getting stuck on a single trajectory.

THE SKILL DAY STRATEGY
The Skill Day Strategy emphasizes organization and focus by dedicating different days of the week to specific areas of development. By following this strategy, musicians can work on multiple skills without feeling overwhelmed, enabling continuous and effective progress towards their goals.

THE FAMILIARITY PRINCIPLE
The Familiarity Principle stresses that as you become more familiar with a given skill, you need less time to practice it. This shift allows for more focus on new skills, preventing plateaus and encouraging continual growth.

THE LAB & FIELD STRATEGY
(Improv for 1/3 to 2/3 of total practice time)
The Lab & Field Strategy divides practice into two parts: the "lab," where you focus on isolated exercises and techniques, and the "field," where you apply those skills by improvising with backing tracks or in real-time musical contexts. This balance ensures you not only perfect your techniques but also learn to use them fluidly in actual musical situations.

THE LISTENER'S SEAT STRATEGY
The Listener's Seat Strategy focuses on recording and listening to your playing, allowing you to objectively evaluate and identify unintentional noises & unwanted tendencies in your playing, and areas for improvement in your performance, songwriting & audio production.

TECHNIQUE DEVELOPMENT

MUSCULAR DEVELOPMENT / PREPAREDNESS / AVOIDING INJURIES
PREPARED MUSCLES STRATEGY
The Prepared Muscles Strategy emphasizes the importance of stretching and properly warming up the muscles before engaging in shred and virtuosic playing. This preparation is vital to ensure comfort, minimize muscle tension, and prevent serious injuries, especially in demanding or cold environments.

RHYTHMIC INVENTORY / AWARENESS & RHYTHMIC FEEL
RHYTHMIC BREATH OF LIFE STRATEGY
(1st goal of anything: make it rhythmic ASAP)
The Rhythmic Breath of Life Strategy emphasizes that the first priority when playing anything is to convert it into a rhythm pattern with clear accenting. By establishing a rhythmic feel from the start, you lay a foundational pulse that brings life to the idea, regardless of tempo.

THE 2 3 4 6 STRATEGY
("Useful Rhythmic Numbers" - Pre-Count Everything!)
The 2 3 4 6 Strategy emphasizes the importance of focusing on the four main rhythmic numbers: 2, 3, 4, and 6, as they form the foundation of most rhythmic situations in music. By concentrating on these quantities, you prepare yourself for the widest possible range of musical contexts, allowing you to pre-count and adapt your playing to different rhythms, aligning with the ShredMentor philosophy of efficient preparation.

THE TREMOLO TRANSFORMATION TECHNIQUE
The Tremolo Transformation Technique involves breaking down a melody into subdivisions based on its shortest rhythmic value and playing everything with tremolo picking. This method helps internalize the exact

length of each note by replacing all sustaining notes with artificial tremolo repetitions.

MUSICALITY

THE CONTINUITY FACTOR
The Continuity Factor emphasizes practicing transitions between phrases and patterns, including the first note of the next section in the current practice. This strategy establishes motor memory for smooth transitions, preventing disjointed and poorly-flowing pieces in your solo or riff, and aids in composing subsequent sections.

SPEED TRAINING

THE 3 SPEEDS STRATEGY
The "3 Speeds Strategy" emphasizes building guitar-playing speed through a three-step approach: starting slow (with concentration), gradually increasing the tempo to the point of falling apart, and then decreasing back to a "tiring" speed where control is regained. This method moves beyond the typical "start slow and speed up" practice, allowing for greater muscle development and control, gradually pushing the controlled speed to higher BPM over time.

THE DEEP END TECHNIQUE
The Deep End Technique challenges conventional wisdom by encouraging you to occasionally start at a fast tempo rather than gradually speeding up. By being "thrown into the deep end," you uncover specific mistakes and tendencies only apparent at faster speeds, enabling you to target and overcome them more effectively.

MOTOR MEMORY PROGRAMMING

THE DEFAULT PICKING STRATEGY
The Default Picking Strategy at ShredMentor encourages defining a consistent picking pattern for each piece, ensuring efficiency and eliminating repetitive decision-making. By focusing on the exact techniques, starting strokes, and pattern length, this strategy enables musicians to effortlessly explore new melodies while reinforcing established playing habits.

THE DEFAULT FINGERING STRATEGY
The Default Fingering Strategy encourages using the same efficient finger combination for a pattern on the guitar whenever possible, eliminating guesswork and aiding muscle memory. This consistent approach promotes effortless playing and allows flexibility for different contexts.

STRENGTH & ENDURANCE
THE TARGETED FINGER COMBINATION STRATEGY
The Targeted Finger Combination Strategy focuses on strengthening the specific finger combinations used in 2-finger and 3-finger scale patterns on the guitar, rather than aimlessly trying to "strengthen your fingers." By practicing these 10 particular combinations, guitarists can efficiently build motor memory and adaptability for various scales and arpeggios, using exercises like rhythmically-counted legato to develop the necessary strength and control.

CONSISTENCY
THE POWER OF 8
(8+ repetitions)
The "Power of 8" Strategy emphasizes achieving consistency and precision by aiming to perform any exercise, sequence, lick, riff, solo, or song at least 8

times in a row without mistakes. If a mistake occurs, the player starts over, possibly slowing down, to complete the 8 repetitions flawlessly, ensuring they are on the right track.

NUANCE / ATTENTION TO DETAIL
THE HANDS SEPARATE STRATEGY
The Hands Separate Strategy involves learning each hand's part individually, enabling awareness of unique challenges without the immediate need for coordination. Common among piano players and valuable for guitarists, this method allows for problem isolation and quicker mastery.

MAXIMUM VERSATILITY
THE COMBINED SKILLS STRATEGY
The Combined Skills Strategy involves practicing multiple guitar skills simultaneously, enhancing individual techniques and the ability to transition between them. By integrating different techniques into complex exercises, guitarists can create more dynamic and engaging music, bridging the gap between isolated practice and real-life performance.

PHRASING & EXPRESSION

ARTICULATION
THE 3 TEXTURES STRATEGY
The "3 Textures" Strategy emphasizes practicing legato, alternate picking, and palm muting together in a single exercise. By cycling through these techniques, guitarists

can seamlessly switch between different expressive "textures" in playing, improvisation, and writing.

OVERALL MUSICALITY
THE ALTERNATING PHRASING STRATEGY
The Alternating Phrasing Strategy focuses on integrating your musical expression into every aspect of practice, turning even speed training and vocabulary development into opportunities for graceful expression through techniques like bending, vibrato, and sliding. By continuously alternating between the technical skill you're working on and the artistic phrasing, you foster immediate adaptation and the ability to fluidly transition between different skills, leading to more passionate and fluent playing.

SCALE & CHORD KNOWLEDGE

PERIPHERAL AWARENESS
THE 3 MODES STRATEGY
The 3 Modes Strategy guides guitarists in practicing a fretboard pattern in three adjacent modes, rather than just one isolated mode. By doing this, musicians overcome the limitation of being stuck in one spot on the fretboard, enhancing their understanding of scale shapes and their transitions, and building motor and visual memory to multiply their results.

THE MULTIPLE LOCATIONS STRATEGY
(Far superior preparedness)
The Multiple Locations Strategy enables musicians to play a melody anywhere on the fretboard, emphasizing practice across all possible permutations to build fluency. Focusing on 3-note-per-string (3NPS) scale

patterns, it allows three potential "shapes" for a melody, fostering greater spontaneity and freedom in expression without reliance on a single form.

THE NOTE LAYOUT STRATEGY

The Note Layout Strategy emphasizes maintaining the same picking pattern across different modes by focusing on the number of notes on each string and the number of strings used, known as the note layout. By keeping this pattern consistent, guitarists can concentrate on the fretting hand's new patterns while still strengthening their picking technique, especially useful for creating new sweep picking patterns, like the commonly used 1+1+2 note layout.

THE SCALE COMPARISON STRATEGY

The Scale Comparison Strategy involves practicing two or more scales alternately to understand their specific differences, acting as "doorways" between the sounds. This systematic method helps in quickly recalling and applying these scales in various musical scenarios, enhancing flexibility and knowledge in scale application.

THE MUSICAL MOTOR MEMORY STRATEGY

The Musical Motor Memory Strategy leverages the natural tendency to play with our fingers first, turning it into an advantage by programming motor memory with actual scales and interval patterns. By practicing the patterns you'll use in real music, rather than random finger exercises, you cultivate a built-in vocabulary that's ready to go, even when creativity doesn't strike immediately.

THE SCALE KNOWLEDGE ONION STRATEGY

The Scale Knowledge Onion Strategy goes far beyond

simply knowing where the notes are on the fretboard and involves a deep understanding of the relationships between notes in a scale. This includes knowledge of scale fragments, intervals, chord formations, arpeggio shapes, note bending, related scales, harmonization, recognizing scales by ear, and more, allowing musicians to use scales more meaningfully and creatively in their playing.

THE CHORD-TYPE ORDER STRATEGY

The Chord-Type Order Strategy helps in recalling the types of chords in a given key, linking each note of a scale to its 3rd and 5th, thus establishing the order of triad chords/arpeggios. It's a part of the Scale Knowledge Onion Strategy, and it aids in recognizing the specific sequence of chord types in different diatonic scales, enabling the musician to focus on practical application rather than memorizing an exhaustive array of musical facts.

THE OBSCURE KEYS STRATEGY

The Obscure Keys Strategy encourages guitarists to explore less familiar keys, specifically those without a root note on any open string, to foster greater fretboard independence. By intentionally practicing in these "obscure" keys, musicians can develop a more versatile skill set and become comfortable recognizing shapes in every key, ultimately enhancing their ability to improvise and adapt to various musical contexts.

THE CHORD PROGRESSION STRATEGY

The Chord Progression Strategy advances beyond methodical adjacent mode practicing by purposely following a chord progression. It emphasizes understanding relationships between non-adjacent modes and works in conjunction with other strategies like the Inversions Strategy to create more natural movement across the fretboard, rather than confining practice to the immediate adjacent modes.

THE BLANK DIAGRAMS STRATEGY
The Blank Diagrams Strategy utilizes blank fretboard diagrams for writing out scale degree numbers, allowing musicians to internalize interval knowledge and understand note relationships without the guitar. This hands-off method helps in developing a deeper understanding of the fretboard and scales, enhancing one's playing ability.

THE INVERSIONS STRATEGY
The Inversions Strategy involves learning multiple forms of a chord, arpeggio, or interval, rather than sticking to one shape, allowing for diverse musical expressions with the same notes. Recognizing that the number of inversions equals the number of different notes in a chord or interval, this method encourages musicians to intentionally practice these inversions, enhancing creativity and flexibility in playing.

THE UNRELATED INSTRUMENT TRANSCRIPTION STRATEGY
The Unrelated Instrument Transcription Strategy involves deliberately learning music written for non-guitar instruments, opening up new pathways on the guitar fretboard. This strategy enhances understanding of the guitar, builds new neural connections, and expands fretboard vocabulary, offering new possibilities and techniques that may not have been considered within the limitations of the guitar's mechanics.

ALWAYS ANALYZING STRATEGY
The Always Analyzing Strategy is an active extension

of musical practice that can be applied throughout daily activities, using environmental sounds as a basis for identifying keys, chords, structures, rhythm, or even humming harmonies to mechanically generated notes. Whether listening to a song while shopping, drumming to the rhythm of a turn signal in traffic, or utilizing natural reverb in a large space, this approach turns ordinary situations into opportunities for constant musical growth and understanding.

CREATIVE & IMPROVISATION SKILLS

THE POWER OF 12
(Re-accenting & repurposing vocabulary)
The "Power of 12" Strategy leverages the multiple facets of 12 to multiply a melody's usability and accenting control in different musical situations. By re-accenting a 12-beat/12-note melody to fit various patterns (such as "Twos," "Threes," "Fours," "Sixes," or alternating odd times), guitarists can expand their vocabulary, improve accenting control, and significantly enhance their concentration, making the melody suitable for various time signatures.

THE GUITAR-LESS COMPOSITION STRATEGY
(Scale degrees, Sequences, Notation, and/or MIDI)
The Guitar-less Composition Strategy provides methods for capturing musical ideas when a guitar is not accessible, ensuring creativity is never lost or altered due to lack of tools. By utilizing ShredMentor Shorthand, traditional music notation, or recording a voice memo, musicians can quickly document ideas, allowing for a greater fluidity in their creative process and the ability to transpose or arrange those ideas later.

3 PARTS STRATEGY
(Songwriting)
The 3 Parts Strategy simplifies songwriting by focusing on creating a verse, chorus, and bridge, allowing for easy arrangement into a structured song. By utilizing tools like chord progression generators and Riffing Styles Tool, musicians can quickly experiment and transform ideas into cohesive music without getting bogged down in details.

THE CALL YOUR POCKET STRATEGY
The Call Your Pocket Strategy draws an analogy from Pool, where improvising is akin to calling a shot, focusing on intentional composition. By verbally identifying specific chord tones (root, 3rd, or 5th) at the start and end of a melody, musicians can enhance their understanding of melody resolution and chord changes.

THE SEQUENCE MANIFESTATIONS STRATEGY
(Technique, Motor Memory, Fretboard Awareness & Music Theory Knowledge, Composition, Improvisation, Intentional Creativity)
Take a single Sequence and apply it, using the exact same rhythmic/accenting criteria, to as many different interval patterns as you can possibly come up with. (This strategy applies to 4 "families" of Interval patterns on the fretboard: 2NPS, 3NPS, 4NPS & Arpeggios; string-skipping and tapping are additionally optional on top of these fretboard pattern "families."

THE CREATIVITY WITH CRITERIA STRATEGY
The Creativity With Criteria Strategy addresses choice paralysis in music composition by narrowing down options through specific criteria. By committing to particular elements like scale, technique, rhythm,

or articulation, musicians can more easily generate creative and high-quality content without becoming overwhelmed by infinite possibilities.

THE CONTAINER METHOD
(Songwriting & Rhythm)
The Container Method involves structuring time in songwriting by selecting a number of measures and filling them with specific rhythmic subdivisions and chord progressions. Like slots in an ice cube tray, each measure can be visualized as a container to be filled, creating a foundation that can be layered and refined, facilitating creativity by giving a starting point and structure.

THE PAINTING WITH SOUND METHOD
The Painting with Sound Method involves creating melodies freely and then adjusting them to fit a rhythm or time signature. This approach allows for a flexible and creative process, where you can add or remove notes and even change time signatures to make your musical idea come to life.

THE CONSOLIDATION STRATEGY
The Consolidation Strategy involves breaking down complex musical passages into sections, then mentally consolidating them into single "things." By practicing this way, you lighten your mental workload, enabling you to perform intricate musical passages without losing your place or feeling overwhelmed.

MIDI-FIRST STRATEGY
The MIDI-First Strategy involves planning out complex guitar solos or songs by entering them as MIDI, allowing you to hear how difficult passages will sound before committing to practicing them, and helps in planning melodies and harmonies without needing to record all

the instruments first. It can save time and reduce stress, letting you focus on composing and then filling in with actual performance and layers afterwards.

RHYTHMIC BUILDING BLOCKS STRATEGY
(unofficially aka Rhythmic "Legos")
The Rhythmic Building Blocks Strategy lets you create complex riffs and solos by stringing together rhythmic phrases, just like snapping together Lego blocks of different sizes. Once assembled, you fill in these rhythmic patterns with musical phrases, allowing for creative and intricate compositions.

CONSTANT VARIATIONS STRATEGY
The Constant Variations Strategy is a powerful way to establish far-reaching fluidity on the instrument, as opposed to the typical "collecting riff/licks" approach so many guitarists use. Instead, the key is to always look for ways to create variations of a given melody. Some of the main tools are Sequences & Offsets, covered extensively in ***The Book of Sequences***, as well as inversion, diminution, augmentation, among others.

RHYTHMIC DOMINOES
(Improvisation/Writing Game)
Rhythmic Dominoes uses a set of dominoes to create a game for improvising and writing music. By using the number values on the random dominoes as rhythmic or phrase criteria, this strategy stimulates creativity and enables you to come up with unique ideas for improvising, soloing, riffing, and songwriting, making it an enjoyable and innovative way to expand your musical skills. Similarly, by using polyhedral dice, you can further gamify additional aspects of musical creativity.

In the following section, I'll expand a bit on one of the most important strategies for your music theory knowledge mentioned above, *The Scale Knowledge Onion*.

THE SCALE KNOWLEDGE...ONION?

This concept developed in 2018 as I was working with a particular student on expanding on just how much the term "scale knowledge" *really* entails.

At the time, I created the graphic below, demonstrating in self-questioning format how to arrive at these additional "layers" of scale knowledge that simply don't even occur to most guitarists.

The thing is, these extra "layers" are SO much more important than "**layer zero**," where most people's scale knowledge starts and ends.

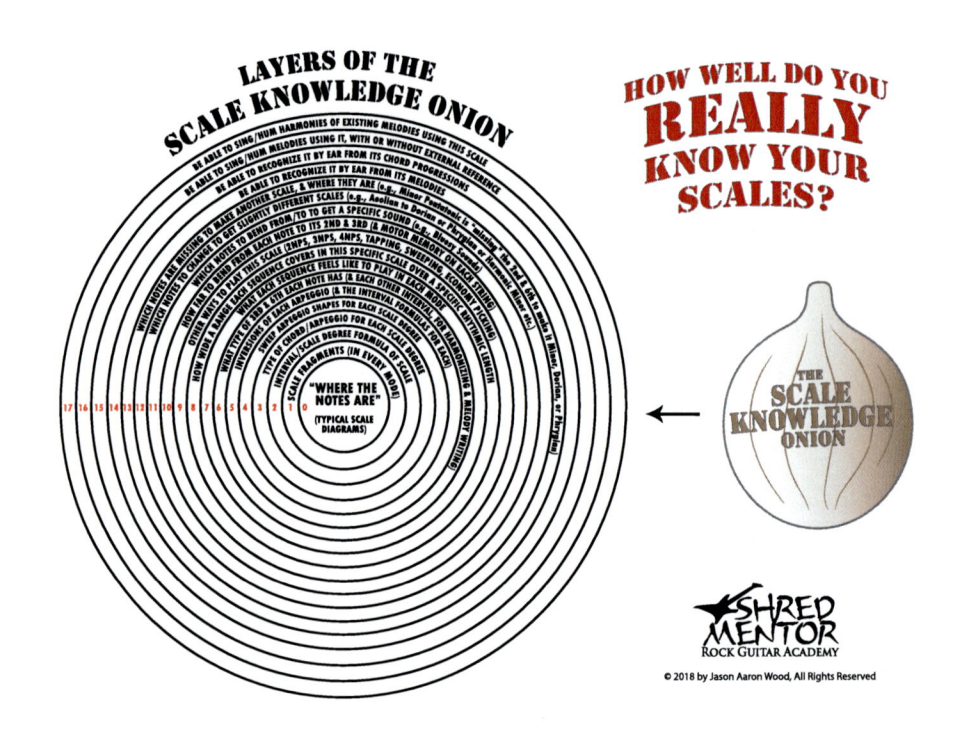

LAYERS OF THE SCALE KNOWLEDGE ONION

- BE ABLE TO SING/HUM HARMONIES OF EXISTING MELODIES USING THIS SCALE
- BE ABLE TO SING/HUM MELODIES USING IT, WITH OR WITHOUT EXTERNAL REFERENCE
- BE ABLE TO RECOGNIZE IT BY EAR FROM ITS CHORD PROGRESSIONS
- BE ABLE TO RECOGNIZE IT BY EAR FROM ITS MELODIES
- BE ABLE TO RECOGNIZE ANOTHER SCALE, & WHERE THEY ARE (e.g., Aeolian to Dorian or Phrygian to Lydian, etc.)
- WHICH NOTES ARE MISSING TO MAKE ANOTHER DIFFERENT SCALES (e.g., Minor Pentatonic is "missing" the 2nd / 6th to make it Blues, Dorian, or Phrygian)
- WHICH NOTES TO CHANGE TO GET SLIGHTLY DIFFERENT SCALES TO GET A SPECIFIC SOUND (e.g., Minor to Harmonic Minor #7)
- HOW A WAY TO BEND FROM/TO ITS 2ND & 3RD (& MOTOR MEMORY OF EACH STRING)
- OTHER NOTES TO BEND FROM EACH NOTE TO ITS 2ND & 3RD (& MOTOR MEMORY OF EACH STRING)
- HOW NOTES FROM THIS SCALE (2NPS, 3NPS, 4NPS, TAPPING, SWEEPING, ECONOMY PICKING
- HOW MANY BACK SEQUENCE COVERS IN THIS SPECIFIC SCALE OVER A SPECIFIC RHYTHMIC LENGTH
- WHAT EACH BACK SEQUENCE FEELS LIKE TO PLAY IN EACH SCALE POSITION
- WHAT TYPE OF 3RD & 5TH EACH NOTE HAS (& EACH OTHER INTERVAL FOR HARMONIZING & MELODY WRITING)
- WHAT TYPE OF ARPEGGIO SHAPES FOR EACH SCALE DEGREE
- SWEEP ARPEGGIO SHAPES FOR EACH SCALE DEGREE
- INVERSIONS OF EACH ARPEGGIO (& THE INTERNAL INTERVALS FOR HARMONIZING & MELODY WRITING)
- INTERVAL/SCALE DEGREE FORMULA OF SCALE
- TYPE OF CHORD/SCALE DEGREE FORMULA OF SCALE
- SCALE FRAGMENTS (IN EVERY MODE)
- **"WHERE THE NOTES ARE"** (TYPICAL SCALE DIAGRAMS)

17 16 15 14 13 12 11 10 9 8 7 6 5 4 3 2 1 0

HOW WELL DO YOU REALLY KNOW YOUR SCALES?

← THE SCALE KNOWLEDGE ONION

SHRED MENTOR ROCK GUITAR ACADEMY

© 2018 by Jason Aaron Wood, All Rights Reserved

84   The Top Secret Book of Practice Routines

Most guitarists' scale knowledge begins and ends at playing the notes of the entire scale ascending and descending across the fretboard, sometimes only in one position (one mode).

This amounts to "which fingers to use" and "where the notes are," which is merely "**step ZERO**" or "**layer zero**" — you haven't even begun yet, since you can't even proceed to do anything musical until you've done at least this much.

In this section, we'll begin exploring further into the many layers of what "scale knowledge" really entails — hence, the Scale Knowledge "Onion" — and in each case, be sure to make it a point to actively develop that aspect of your scale knowledge

- (a) on the fretboard in your practice time,
- (b) when improvising and
- (c) when composing music for your own songs.

THE "LAYERS" OF *TRUE* SCALE KNOWLEDGE

In the years since I first brainstormed the layers of scale knowledge for the original graphic, I inevitably thought of a few more important layers.

So, to save your eyes some strain (given how small the text is on that graphic) and to equip you with the types of things you really need to know when you learn a scale, here is the current list of the Layers of Scale Knowledge, specifically for guitarists:

→ What is the interval pattern of a specific scale fragment [trichord, tetrachord, pentachord, hexachord] from each mode/scale degree of a given scale?

And what finger combination would you use by default to play it?

→ What is the interval pattern (note spacing) of this scale?

→ What is the scale degree formula of this scale based on the numbering of the Major scale? (1 2 3 4 5 6 7) [ie, which notes are sharp and/or flat?]

→ What type of triad occurs at each scale degree of this scale? What type of 7th chord?

→ What are the arpeggio shapes for each triad in this scale? (Sweep AND non-sweep) What about 7ths?

→ When you play an arpeggio from each mode in this scale, where are all of the other surrounding scale tones under your hand when you play it, if you wanted to add an in-key passing tone?

→ Which 3 triads is each note of the scale (each scale degree) contained in (as the root, the 3rd, and the 5th of that chord)? For example, which 3 chords contain the 2nd of the scale and what type of chord is each one?

→ What are the inversion shapes of each arpeggio at each scale degree of this scale? What is the interval pattern of each of these arpeggio inversions?
→ What type of 3rd and 6th does each note in this scale have? (and each other interval as well for harmonizing purposes)

→ What does each Sequence feel like to play in each mode of the scale, and how does it change the finger combination you use and what stretching is involved if any? (Scale/fretboard knowledge meets motor memory/technique)

→ How wide a range of notes does each Sequence span in this specific scale over a specific rhythmic length? (be specific: "if I start HERE playing [sequence] at [sub-beat value] for [# of beats], I will end [where?]")

→ What other ways can I approach playing this scale on the guitar? (2NPS, 3NPS, 4NPS, Tapping, Sweeping, Economy Picking, String-Skipping, etc)

→ How far do I need to bend from each note in this scale to its 2nd or 3rd? (Motor memory & string tension knowledge)

→ Which notes in this scale do I bend to/from to get a certain sound or character (e.g., Bluesy Sounds)?

→ Which notes do I change in this scale to get a slightly different scale, and what new key does that put me in? (e.g., from Aeolian to Dorian or Phrygian or Harmonic Minor) Which notes, and in which direction are they moved, up or down?

→ Which notes are *missing* from this scale to make it another scale?

    (e.g., Minor pentatonic: how do I make it Aeolian? Dorian? Phrygian?... Hirojoshi: how do I make it Aeolian? Harmonic Minor? Hungarian Minor?)

AWAY FROM THE GUITAR:

→ How well can I program melodies using this scale in MIDI using the Piano Roll in my DAW? What about in keys other than

A minor / C major?

→ Am I able to recognize this scale from a melody I'm hearing?

→ Am I able to recognize what type of scale this is based on a chord progression?

→ Am I able to sing or hum a melody using this scale, with or without an external reference pitch?

→ Am I able to sing or hum harmonies of existing melodies using this scale?

44 ESSENTIAL QUESTIONS
TO ASK YOURSELF DURING PLAYING & PRACTICING

In the same spirit as the previous section, I want to similarly draw your attention to things that you should be thinking about in general whenever you're practicing.

One of the biggest factors in how much progress you make, and how quickly, is the **QUALITY OF YOUR CONCENTRATION**, as well as the **CRITERIA** that you're using when evaluating how well you're doing as you play.

Now, hopefully your current practice doesn't consist of merely "*going through the motions*" like so many other guitar players often do.

But if that IS the case, rest assured that you'll start to notice some significant improvements in your productivity once you begin internalizing these 44 questions.

Remember: Advanced guitar playing demands a very high level of concentration.

From now on, remember to continually ask yourself the following questions until they become things you naturally look for in your playing:

FRETTING HAND:

1. Are my fingers moving TOO FAR AWAY FROM THE STRINGS (ie, more than ½") when not in use?

2. Am I using ONLY my fingerTIPS to press down the strings?

3. Am I pressing down HARD ENOUGH on the strings to get a clean sound?

4. Am I pressing down TOO HARD?

5. Am I using JUST ENOUGH of the finger to get a GOOD SOUND without being INEFFICIENT?

6. Are my notes RINGING OUT FULLY, until the next note begins?

7. Are my notes RINGING CLEANLY, with no fret buzz or choked strings from other fingers hitting them?

8. Am I getting a FULL, CLEAN SOUND ON *EVERY NOTE*?

9. Are my notes ON-PITCH, or am I supporting the weight of my arm by "hanging" on the strings from my fingertips, causing the strings to bend downward and raise the pitch of my notes?

10. Are my fingers SPRINGING OFF THE STRING AS QUICKLY AS POSSIBLE, without cutting off the sound?

11. Is my THUMB correctly positioned in the CENTER of the REAR of the neck, with the flat of the tip just opposite my middle finger? (Note: this does not apply when performing string bending.)

12. Is more of my THUMB coming in contact with the rear of the neck than necessary, causing EXCESS FRICTION and DECREASING MOBILITY?

13. Are my hammer-ons and pull-offs of EQUAL VOLUME on

ALL 4 FRETTING FINGERS?

14. (This is also related to EAR TRAINING) When BENDING, am I bending EXACTLY to my TARGET PITCH, or am I bending a little bit sharp or flat?

PICKING HAND:

15. Am I picking with the LEAST AMOUNT OF MOVEMENT necessary?

16. Am I using ONLY THE TIP OF THE PICK to pluck the strings?

17. Am I picking FROM THE WRIST, or is my picking motion coming from the elbow or fingers?

18. Am I playing ONLY my INTENDED NOTES, or is there additional string noise when moving from one string to the next?

19. When Alternate Picking is called for (that is, in most cases), am I using it consistently, or am I repeating downstrokes or upstrokes consecutively?

20. Is my picking EXACTLY IN TIME with the music, or is there consistent variation between my picking and the beat?

21. When picking FAST, am I able to keep count, or AM I PICKING FASTER THAN I CAN CONCENTRATE (this is called "flailing")?

22. Am I ACCENTING the first note of each tuplet grouping, or are all of my notes sort of blending together with no dynamics to prioritize notes falling on important beats?

23. What is the time signature and rhythmic subdivision of

what I am playing (or playing along to)?

24. Without intentionally accenting, are my DOWNSTROKES and UPSTROKES *EVEN IN VOLUME*?

SYNCHRONIZATION & COORDINATION BETWEEN BOTH HANDS:

25. Are my LEFT AND RIGHT hands working TOGETHER perfectly in sync with each other?

FOCUS AND CONCENTRATION:

26. Is my practice environment free from EXTERNAL DISTRACTIONS, like TV, phone calls, notifications, or texts, social media, email, etc.?

27. Am I concentrating 100% on WHAT I'M PLAYING, or is my mind wandering or focusing on other things?

MUSICAL USEFULNESS OF WHAT YOU'RE PRACTICING:

28. Am I playing an endless, aimless string of notes, or a rhythmic phrase with clear accenting?

29. *What is the total number of notes that should be in this phrase* in order to accent it to fit into this time signature/accenting pattern?

30. What specific type of scale is what I am playing based on?

(e.g., natural minor, harmonic minor, minor pentatonic, whole tone scale, etc.)

31. What does this exercise look, sound, and feel like in the next higher or lower mode in the same scale, and how do I need to adjust which fingers I'm using to account for the different interval spacing?

32. If I break this melody down into a _sequence_, how can I apply that sequence to
another type of fretboard pattern that contains the same number of notes?

33. How else might I be able to re-accent what I'm playing in order to use it in different rhythmic situations? (ie, in what other rhythmic contexts, subdivision values or time signatures?)

34. Where else on the fretboard can I play this same exact melody with a different note layout (the same notes on different strings)?

35. How well does this work when I play it along to backing tracks?

36. What are the notes that make up each chord in the backing track, and where are those notes in the fretboard pattern I'm playing so that I can resolve my melodies?

QUALITY OF TIME MANAGEMENT:

37. What are my _top 5 to 10 highest-priority skills_ that I want to develop, and how many can I fit into a 1-hour practice routine if I spend 10 minutes on each one?

38. How many of those skills can I combine intentionally into "one exercise" so I can specifically practice _using them together, while taking up less of my overall practice time on_

each one separately?

39. Am I spending too much time on this single exercise & squandering time I could spend on also developing additional skills today? (ie, just how much better am I really going to get at this skill TODAY, as opposed to this week if I do it every day?)

40. Am I making it a point to apply this along to a backing track (aka, musically) at least 1/3 of the time, or am I just in "exercise mode" all the time?

41. Are the things I'm practicing only staying within my comfort zone, or am I reaching for things to intentionally challenge me (ie, ultimately *expanding* my comfort zone)?

42. Am I losing progress on the things I'm already good at by only focusing on new things, or am I also making time for "maintenance" of my existing skills?

43. Am I going into my practice routine every time with a clear (written) game plan — or better yet, a strategy for achieving my goals — or am I wandering aimlessly from one skill to the next and just "winging it" from one moment to the next as I go?

44. With the way I'm practicing, am I actually building a working vocabulary that I can use a wide variety of situations, or am I just "collecting" TABs and exercises?

INTERNALIZE

As you continue to progress on the guitar, try to internalize these 44 questions and look for these things each time you play.

About the Author

When he's not teaching ShredMentor students, or creating ShredMentor backing tracks & practice tools, guitarist & composer **Jason Aaron Wood** is usually working on his next album release for his self-titled solo project, his other solo project **Ol Sonuf**, or working with his wife & long-time bandmate **Laurie Ann Haus** on music for their band **Todesbonden**.

Frustrated by the slow progress that comes with outdated, traditional teaching styles, in 2008 Jason created ShredMentor Rock Guitar Academy, creating a results-based system of personalized teaching, & amassing a collection of the most hard-hitting, high-yield activities he'd discovered since starting on the guitar in 1992, while simultaneously weeding out the many ineffective practice methods that most guitarists think they're supposed to follow.

As the creator of 2 separate one-man bands, Jason has released 6 solo albums in the span of 6 years, while being hired for an ever-growing number of guest solos, & continues to push the boundaries of his own playing, songwriting, & overall musicianship using the same principles he teaches under the ShredMentor banner, & using the same Guitar Practice Tools he developed for his students in his own practice.

You can find his solo albums on his Bandcamp page: jasonaaronwood.bandcamp.com and Todesbonden's music on their Bandcamp page: todesbonden.bandcamp.com

Other Books to Improve Your Musicianship

The Book of Sequences

1,001 Guitar Practice Ideas

The ShredMentor Strategies

The Solo Writing Notebook

The Sequence Workbook

Practicing For Results

The Sweep Picking Visual Guide

The 8-String Book
Vol. 1: Scales & Modes

The 8-String Book
Vol. 2: Sweep Arpeggios

Made in the USA
Monee, IL
03 January 2025

524d8c41-ff0a-44e0-bcfb-ffd5314dd8feR01